'O let them be
left, wild
and wet

GERARD MANLEY HOPKINS
Born 1844, Essex, England
Died 1889, Dublin, Ireland

Hopkins's poems were first published posthumously in 1918,
in a volume edited by his friend, the poet Robert Bridges.

HOPKINS IN PENGUIN CLASSICS
Poems and Prose

GERARD MANLEY HOPKINS

As king fishers catch fire

PENGUIN BOOKS

PENGUIN CLASSICS

Published by the Penguin Group
Penguin Books Ltd, 80 Strand, London WC2R 0RL, England
Penguin Group (USA) Inc., 375 Hudson Street, New York, New York 10014, USA
Penguin Group (Canada), 90 Eglinton Avenue East, Suite 700, Toronto,
Ontario, Canada M4P 2Y3 (a division of Pearson Penguin Canada Inc.)
Penguin Ireland, 25 St Stephen's Green, Dublin 2, Ireland
(a division of Penguin Books Ltd)
Penguin Group (Australia), 707 Collins Street, Melbourne, Victoria 3008, Australia
(a division of Pearson Australia Group Pty Ltd)
Penguin Books India Pvt Ltd, 11 Community Centre, Panchsheel Park,
New Delhi – 110 017, India
Penguin Group (NZ), 67 Apollo Drive, Rosedale, Auckland 0632, New Zealand
(a division of Pearson New Zealand Ltd)
Penguin Books (South Africa) (Pty) Ltd, Block D, Rosebank Office Park,
181 Jan Smuts Avenue, Parktown North, Gauteng 2193, South Africa

Penguin Books Ltd, Registered Offices: 80 Strand, London WC2R 0RL, England

www.penguin.com

This selection published in Penguin Classics 2015
001

Set in 9.5/13 pt Baskerville 10 Pro
Typeset by Jouve (UK), Milton Keynes
Printed in Great Britain by Clays Ltd, St Ives plc

A CIP catalogue record for this book is available from the British Library

ISBN: 978-0-141-39784-9

www.greenpenguin.co.uk

MIX
Paper from
responsible sources
FSC
www.fsc.org   FSC® C018179

Penguin Books is committed to a sustainable
future for our business, our readers and our planet.
This book is made from Forest Stewardship
Council™ certified paper.

Contents

God's Grandeur

The world is charged with the grandeur of God.
    It will flame out, like shining from shook foil;
    It gathers to a greatness, like the ooze of oil
Crushed. Why do men then now not reck his rod?
Generations have trod, have trod, have trod;
    And all is seared with trade; bleared, smeared with
        toil;
    And wears man's smudge and shares man's smell:
        the soil
Is bare now, nor can foot feel, being shod.

And for all this, nature is never spent;
    There lives the dearest freshness deep down things;
And though the last lights off the black West went
    Oh, morning, at the brown brink eastward, springs –
Because the Holy Ghost over the bent
    World broods with warm breast and with ah! bright
        wings.

The Starlight Night

Look at the stars! look, look up at the skies!
   O look at all the fire-folk sitting in the air!
   The bright boroughs, the circle-citadels there!
Down in dim woods the diamond delves! the
      elves'-eyes!
The grey lawns cold where gold, where quickgold lies!
   Wind-beat whitebeam! airy abeles set on a flare!
   Flake-doves sent floating forth at a farmyard scare!
Ah well! it is all a purchase, all is a prize.

Buy then! bid then! – What? Prayer, patience, alms,
      vows.
Look, look: a May-mess, like on orchard boughs!
   Look! March-bloom, like on mealed-with-yellow
      sallows!
These are indeed the barn; withindoors house
The shocks. This piece-bright paling shuts the spouse
   Christ home, Christ and his mother and all his
      hallows.

'As kingfishers catch fire'

As kingfishers catch fire, dragonflies draw flame;
As tumbled over rim in roundy wells
Stones ring; like each tucked string tells, each hung
     bell's
Bow swung finds tongue to fling out broad its name;
Each mortal thing does one thing and the same:
Deals out that being indoors each one dwells;
Selves – goes itself; *myself* it speaks and spells,
Crying *Whát I dó is me: for that I came.*

I say móre: the just man justices;
Keeps gráce: thát keeps all his goings graces;
Acts in God's eye what in God's eye he is –
Chríst – for Christ plays in ten thousand places,
Lovely in limbs, and lovely in eyes not his
To the Father through the features of men's faces.

Spring

Nothing is so beautiful as Spring –
　　When weeds, in wheels, shoot long and lovely and
　　　lush;
　　Thrush's eggs look little low heavens, and thrush
Through the echoing timber does so rinse and wring
The ear, it strikes like lightnings to hear him sing;
　　The glassy peartree leaves and blooms, they brush
　　The descending blue; that blue is all in a rush
With richness; the racing lambs too have fair their fling.

What is all this juice and all this joy?
　　A strain of the earth's sweet being in the beginning
In Eden garden. – Have, get, before it cloy,
　　Before it cloud, Christ, lord, and sour with sinning,
Innocent mind and Mayday in girl and boy,
　　Most, O maid's child, thy choice and worthy the
　　　winning.

The Lantern Out of Doors

Sometimes a lantern moves along the night,
    That interests our eyes. And who goes there?
    I think; where from and bound, I wonder, where,
With, all down darkness wide, his wading light?

Men go by me whom either beauty bright
    In mould or mind or what not else makes rare:
    They rain against our much-thick and marsh air
Rich beams, till death or distance buys them quite.

Death or distance soon consumes them: wind
    What most I may eye after, be in at the end
I cannot, and out of sight is out of mind.

Christ minds: Christ's interest, what to avow or amend
    There, éyes them, heart wánts, care haúnts, foot fóllows
        kínd,
Their ránsom, théir rescue, ánd first, fást, last friénd.

The Sea and the Skylark

On ear and ear two noises too old to end
    Trench – right, the tide that ramps against the shore;
    With a flood or a fall, low lull-off or all roar,
Frequenting there while moon shall wear and wend.

Left hand, off land, I hear the lark ascend,
    His rash-fresh re-winded new-skeinèd score
    In crisps of curl off wild winch whirl, and pour
And pelt music, till none's to spill nor spend.

How these two shame this shallow and frail town!
    How ring right out our sordid turbid time,
Being pure! We, life's pride and cared-for crown,

    Have lost that cheer and charm of earth's past prime:
Our make and making break, are breaking, down
    To man's last dust, drain fast towards man's first slime.

The Windhover

to Christ our Lord

I caught this morning morning's minion, king-
  dom of daylight's dauphin, dapple-dawn-drawn
  Falcon, in his riding
Of the rolling level underneath him steady air, and
  striding
High there, how he rung upon the rein of a wimpling wing
In his ecstasy! then off, off forth on swing,
  As a skate's heel sweeps smooth on a bow-bend: the hurl
  and gliding
Rebuffed the big wind. My heart in hiding
Stirred for a bird, – the achieve of, the mastery of the thing!

Brute beauty and valour and act, oh, air, pride, plume, here
  Buckle! AND the fire that breaks from thee then, a billion
Times told lovelier, more dangerous. O my chevalier!

  No wonder of it: shéer plód makes plough down sillion
Shine, and blue-bleak embers, ah my dear,
  Fall, gall themselves, and gash gold-vermilion.

Pied Beauty

Glory be to God for dappled things –
    For skies of couple-colour as a brinded cow;
      For rose-moles in all stipple upon trout that swim;
Fresh-firecoal chestnut-falls; finches' wings;
    Landscape plotted and pieced – fold, fallow, and
        plough;
      And áll trádes, their gear and tackle and trim.

All things counter, original, spare, strange;
    Whatever is fickle, freckled (who knows how?)
      With swift, slow; sweet, sour; adazzle, dim;
He fathers-forth whose beauty is past change:
        Praise him.

Hurrahing in Harvest

Summer ends now; now, barbarous in beauty, the
    stooks rise
  Around; up above, what wind-walks! what lovely
    behaviour
  Of silk-sack clouds! has wilder, wilful-wavier
Meal-drift moulded ever and melted across skies?

I walk, I lift up, I lift up heart, eyes,
  Down all that glory in the heavens to glean our
    Saviour;
  And, éyes, heárt, what looks, what lips yet gave you a
Rapturous love's greeting of realer, of rounder replies?

And the azurous hung hills are his world-wielding
    shoulder
  Majestic – as a stallion stalwart, very-violet-sweet! –
These things, these things were here and but the beholder
  Wanting; which two when they once meet,
The heart réars wíngs bold and bolder
  And hurls for him, O half hurls earth for him off
    under his feet.

9

The Caged Skylark

As a dare-gale skylark scanted in a dull cage
    Man's mounting spirit in his bone-house, mean
      house, dwells –
    That bird beyond the remembering his free fells;
This in drudgery, day-labouring-out life's age.

Though aloft on turf or perch or poor low stage,
    Both sing sometímes the sweetest, sweetest spells,
    Yet both droop deadly sómetimes in their cells
Or wring their barriers in bursts of fear or rage.

Not that the sweet-fowl, song-fowl, needs no rest –
Why, hear him, hear him babble and drop down to
      his nest,
    But his own nest, wild nest, no prison.

Man's spirit will be flesh-bound when found at best,
But uncumberèd: meadow-down is not distressed
    For a rainbow footing it nor he for his bónes rísen.

In the Valley of the Elwy

I remember a house where all were good
　　To me, God knows, deserving no such thing:
　　Comforting smell breathed at very entering,
Fetched fresh, as I suppose, off some sweet wood.
That cordial air made those kind people a hood
　　All over, as a bevy of eggs the mothering wing
　　Will, or mild nights the new morsels of Spring:
Why, it seemed of course; seemed of right it should.

Lovely the woods, waters, meadows, combes, vales,
All the air things wear that build this world of Wales;
　　Only the inmate does not correspond:
God, lover of souls, swaying considerate scales,
Complete thy creature dear O where it fails,
　　Being mighty a master, being a father and fond.

Binsey Poplars

felled 1879

My aspens dear, whose airy cages quelled,
Quelled or quenched in leaves the leaping sun,
All felled, felled, are all felled;
   Of a fresh and following folded rank
       Not spared, not one
       That dandled a sandalled
     Shadow that swam or sank
On meadow and river and wind-wandering weed-
   winding bank.

O if we but knew what we do
     When we delve or hew –
   Hack and rack the growing green!
     Since country is so tender
   To touch, her being só slender,
   That, like this sleek and seeing ball
   But a prick will make no eye at all,
   Where we, even where we mean

To mend her we end her,
When we hew or delve:
After-comers cannot guess the beauty been.
Ten or twelve, only ten or twelve
Strokes of havoc únselve
The sweet especial scene,
Rural scene, a rural scene,
Sweet especial rural scene.

Duns Scotus's Oxford

Towery city and branchy between towers;
Cuckoo-echoing, bell-swarmèd, lark-charmèd,
    rook-racked, river-rounded;
The dapple-eared lily below thee; that country and
    town did
Once encounter in, here coped and poisèd powers;

Thou hast a base and brickish skirt there, sours
That neighbour-nature thy grey beauty is grounded
Best in; graceless growth, thou hast confounded
Rural rural keeping – folk, flocks, and flowers.

Yet ah! this air I gather and I release
He lived on; these weeds and waters, these walls are
    what
He haunted who of all men most sways my spirits to
    peace;

Of realty the rarest-veinèd unraveller; a not
Rivalled insight, be rival Italy or Greece;
Who fired France for Mary without spot.

Peace

When will you ever, Peace, wild wooddove, shy wings
    shut,
Your round me roaming end, and under be my boughs?
When, when, Peace, will you, Peace? I'll not play
    hypocrite
To own my heart: I yield you do come sometimes; but
That piecemeal peace is poor peace. What pure peace
    allows
Alarms of wars, the daunting wars, the death of it?

O surely, reaving Peace, my Lord should leave in lieu
Some good! And so he does leave Patience exquisite,
That plumes to Peace thereafter. And when Peace here
    does house
He comes with work to do, he does not come to coo,
        He comes to brood and sit.

The Candle Indoors

Some candle clear burns somewhere I come by.
I muse at how its being puts blissful back
With yellowy moisture mild night's blear-all black,
Or to-fro tender trambeams truckle at the eye.
By that window what task what fingers ply,
I plod wondering, a-wanting, just for lack
Of answer the eagerer a-wanting Jessy or Jack
There / God to aggrándise, God to glorify. –

Come you indoors, come home; your fading fire
Mend first and vital candle in close heart's vault:
You there are master, do your own desire;
What hinders? Are you beam-blind, yet to a fault
In a neighbour deft-handed? are you that liar
And, cast by conscience out, spendsavour salt?

At the Wedding March

God with honour hang your head,
Groom, and grace you, bride, your bed
With lissome scions, sweet scions,
Out of hallowed bodies bred.

Each be other's comfort kind:
Déep, déeper than divined,
Divine charity, dear charity,
Fast you ever, fast bind.

Then let the March tread our ears:
I to him turn with tears
Who to wedlock, his wonder wedlock,
Déals tríumph and immortal years.

Felix Randal

Felix Randal the farrier, O is he dead then? my duty
  all ended,
Who have watched his mould of man, big-boned and
  hardy-handsome
Pining, pining, till time when reason rambled in it
  and some
Fatal four disorders, fleshed there, all contended?

Sickness broke him. Impatient, he cursed at first,
  but mended
Being anointed and all; though a heavenlier heart
  began some
Months earlier, since I had our sweet reprieve and
  ransom
Tendered to him. Ah well, God rest him all road
  ever he offended!

This seeing the sick endears them to us, us too it
  endears.
My tongue had taught thee comfort, touch had
  quenched thy tears,
Thy tears that touched my heart, child, Felix, poor
  Felix Randal;

How far from then forethought of, all thy more
    boisterous years,
When thou at the random grim forge, powerful amidst
    peers,
Didst fettle for the great grey drayhorse his bright and
    battering sandal!

Spring and Fall

to a young child

Márgarét, áre you gríeving
Over Goldengrove unleaving?
Leáves líke the things of man, you
With your fresh thoughts care for, can you?
Ah! ás the heart grows older
It will come to such sights colder
By and by, nor spare a sigh
Though worlds of wanwood leafmeal lie;
And yet you will weep and know why.
Now no matter, child, the name:
Sórrow's spríngs áre the same.
Nor mouth had, no nor mind, expressed
What heart heard of, ghost guessed:
It ís the blight man was born for,
It is Margaret you mourn for.

Inversnaid

This darksome burn, horseback brown,
His rollrock highroad roaring down,
In coop and in comb the fleece of his foam
Flutes and low to the lake falls home.

A windpuff-bonnet of fáwn-fróth
Turns and twindles over the broth
Of a pool so pitchblack, féll-frówning,
It rounds and rounds Despair to drowning.

Degged with dew, dappled with dew
Are the groins of the braes that the brook treads
    through,
Wiry heathpacks, flitches of fern,
And the beadbonny ash that sits over the burn.

What would the world be, once bereft
Of wet and of wilderness? Let them be left,
O let them be left, wildness and wet;
Long live the weeds and the wilderness yet.

The Leaden Echo and the Golden Echo

(Maiden's song from St Winefred's Well)

THE LEADEN ECHO

How to kéep – is there ány any, is there none such,
    nowhere known some, bow or brooch or braid or
    brace, láce, latch or catch or key to keep
Back beauty, keep it, beauty, beauty, beauty, . . . from
    vanishing away?
Ó is there no frowning of these wrinkles, rankèd
    wrinkles deep,
Dówn? no waving off of these most mournful
    messengers, still messengers, sad and stealing
    messengers of grey?
No there's none, there's none, O no there's none,
Nor can you long be, what you now are, called fair,
Do what you may do, what, do what you may,
And wisdom is early to despair:
Be beginning; since, no, nothing can be done
To keep at bay
Age and age's evils, hoar hair,
Ruck and wrinkle, drooping, dying, death's worst,
    winding sheets, tombs and worms and tumbling
    to decay;

So be beginning, be beginning to despair.
O there's none; no no no there's none:
Be beginning to despair, to despair,
Despair, despair, despair, despair.

THE GOLDEN ECHO

      Spare!
There ís one, yes I have one (Hush there!);
Only not within seeing of the sun,
Not within the singeing of the strong sun,
Tall sun's tingeing, or treacherous the tainting of the
    earth's air,
Somewhere elsewhere there is ah well where! one,
Óne. Yes I cán tell such a key, I dó know such a place,
Where whatever's prized and passes of us, everything
    that's fresh and fast flying of us, seems to us sweet
    of us and swiftly away with, done away with,
    undone,
Úndone, done with, soon done with, and yet dearly and
    dangerously sweet
Of us, the wimpled-water-dimpled, not-by-morning-
    matchèd face,
The flower of beauty, fleece of beauty, too too apt to,
    ah! to fleet,
Never fleets móre, fastened with the tenderest truth

To its own best being and its loveliness of youth: it is an
	everlastingness of, O it is an all youth!
Come then, your ways and airs and looks, locks, maiden
	gear, gallantry and gaiety and grace,
Winning ways, airs innocent, maiden manners, sweet
	looks, loose locks, long locks, lovelocks, gaygear,
	going gallant, girlgrace –
Resign them, sign them, seal them, send them, motion
	them with breath,
And with sighs soaring, soaring síghs deliver
Them; beauty-in-the-ghost, deliver it, early now, long
	before death
Give beauty back, beauty, beauty, beauty, back to God,
	beauty's self and beauty's giver.
See; not a hair is, not an eyelash, not the least lash lost;
	every hair
Is, hair of the head, numbered.
Nay, what we had lighthanded left in surly the mere
	mould
Will have waked and have waxed and have walked with
	the wind what while we slept,
This side, that side hurling a heavyheaded hundredfold
What while we, while we slumbered.
O then, weary then whý should we tread? O why are we
	so haggard at the heart, so care-coiled, care-killed, so
	fagged, so fashed, so cogged, so cumbered,
When the thing we freely fórfeit is kept with fonder a care,
Fonder a care kept than we could have kept it, kept

Far with fonder a care (and we, we should have lost it)
    finer, fonder
A care kept. – Where kept? Do but tell us where kept, where. –
Yonder. – What high as that! We follow, now we follow. –
    Yonder, yes yonder, yonder,
Yonder.

'To seem the stranger'

To seem the stranger lies my lot, my life
Among strangers. Father and mother dear,
Brothers and sisters are in Christ not near
And he my peace/my parting, sword and strife.

England, whose honour O all my heart woos, wife
To my creating thought, would neither hear
Me, were I pleading, plead nor do I: I wear-
y of idle a being but by where wars are rife.

I am in Ireland now; now I am at a third
Remove. Not but in all removes I can
Kind love both give and get. Only what word
Wisest my heart breeds dark heaven's baffling ban
Bars or hell's spell thwarts. This to hoard unheard,
Heard unheeded, leaves me a lonely began.

'I wake and feel'

I wake and feel the fell of dark, not day.
What hours, O what black hours we have spent
This night! what sights you, heart, saw; ways you went!
And more must, in yet longer light's delay.

  With witness I speak this. But where I say
Hours I mean years, mean life. And my lament
Is cries countless, cries like dead letters sent
To dearest him that lives alas! away.

    I am gall, I am heartburn. God's most deep decree
Bitter would have me taste: my taste was me;
Bones built in me, flesh filled, blood brimmed the curse.
    Selfyeast of spirit a dull dough sours. I see
The lost are like this, and their scourge to be
As I am mine, their sweating selves; but worse.

'No worst'

No worst, there is none. Pitched past pitch of grief,
More pangs will, schooled at forepangs, wilder wring.
Comforter, where, where is your comforting?
Mary, mother of us, where is your relief?
My cries heave, herds-long; huddle in a main, a chief
Woe, wórld-sorrow; on an áge-old anvil wince and sing –
Then lull, then leave off. Fury had shrieked 'No ling-
ering! Let me be fell: force I must be brief'.

O the mind, mind has mountains; cliffs of fall
Frightful, sheer, no-man-fathomed. Hold them cheap
May who ne'er hung there. Nor does long our small
Durance deal with that steep or deep. Here! creep,
Wretch, under a comfort serves in a whirlwind: all
Life death does end and each day dies with sleep.

(*Carrion Comfort*)

Not, I'll not, carrion comfort, Despair, not feast on thee;
Not untwist – slack they may be – these last strands
    of man
In me ór, most weary, cry *I can no more*. I can;
Can something, hope, wish day come, not choose
    not to be.
But ah, but O thou terrible, why wouldst thou rude
    on me
Thy wring-world right foot rock? lay a lionlimb against
    me? scan
With darksome devouring eyes my bruisèd bones?
    and fan,
O in turns of tempest, me heaped there; me frantic to
    avoid thee and flee?

   Why? That my chaff might fly; my grain lie, sheer
    and clear.
Nay in all that toil, that coil, since (seems) I kissed
    the rod,
Hand rather, my heart lo! lapped strength, stole joy,
    would laugh, chéer.
Cheer whom though? the hero whose heaven-handling
    flung me, fóot tród

Me? or me that fought him? O which one? is it each
    one? That night, that year
Of now done darkness I wretch lay wrestling with
    (my God!) my God.

'Patience, hard thing'

Patience, hard thing! the hard thing but to pray,
But bid for, Patience is! Patience who asks
Wants war, wants wounds; weary his times, his tasks;
To do without, take tosses, and obey.
    Rare patience roots in these, and, these away,
Nowhere. Natural heart's ivy, Patience masks
Our ruins of wrecked past purpose. There she basks
Purple eyes and seas of liquid leaves all day.

We hear our hearts grate on themselves: it kills
To bruise them dearer. Yet the rebellious wills
Of us we do bid God bend to him even so.
    And where is he who more and more distils
Delicious kindness? – He is patient. Patience fills
His crisp combs, and that comes those ways we know.

'My own heart'

My own heart let me more have pity on; let
Me live to my sad self hereafter kind,
Charitable; not live this tormented mind
With this tormented mind tormenting yet.
    I cast for comfort I can no more get
By groping round my comfortless, than blind
Eyes in their dark can day or thirst can find
Thirst's all-in-all in all a world of wet.

Soul, self; come, poor Jackself, I do advise
You, jaded, let be; call off thoughts awhile
Elsewhere; leave comfort root-room; let joy size
At God knows when to God knows what; whose smile
's not wrung, see you; unforeseen times rather – as skies
Betweenpie mountains – lights a lovely mile.

Spelt from Sibyl's Leaves

Earnest, earthless, equal, attuneable, ' vaulty,
  voluminous, . . . stupendous
Evening strains to be time's vást, ' womb-of-all, home-
  of-all, hearse-of-all night.
Her fond yellow hornlight wound to the west, ' her wild
  hollow hoarlight hung to the height
Waste; her earliest stars, earl-stars, ' stárs principal,
  overbend us,
Fíre-féaturing heaven. For earth ' her being has
  unbound, her dapple is at an end, as-
tray or aswarm, all throughther, in throngs; ' self ín self
  steepèd and páshed – qúite
Disremembering, dísmémbering ' áll now. Heart, you
  round me right
With: Óur évening is over us; óur night ' whélms,
  whélms, ánd will end us.
Only the beak-leaved boughs dragonish ' damask the
  tool-smooth bleak light; black,
Ever so black on it. Óur tale, O óur oracle! ' Lét life,
  wáned, ah lét life wind
Off hér once skéined stained véined varíety ' upon, áll
  on twó spools; párt, pen, páck
Now her áll in twó flocks, twó folds – black, white; '
  right, wrong; reckon but, reck but, mind

33

But thése two; wáre of a wórld where bút these ' twó
     tell, each off the óther; of a rack
Where, selfwrung, selfstrung, sheathe- and shelterless, '
     thóughts agaínst thoughts ín groans grínd.

That Nature is a Heraclitean Fire and of the Comfort of the Resurrection

Cloud-puffball, torn tufts, tossed pillows ' flaunt forth,
    then chevy on an air-
built thoroughfare: heaven-roysterers, in gay-gangs '
    they throng; they glitter in marches.
Down roughcast, down dazzling whitewash, ' wherever
    an elm arches,
Shivelights and shadowtackle in long ' lashes lace,
    lance, and pair.
Delightfully the bright wind boisterous ' ropes,
    wrestles, beats earth bare
Of yestertempest's creases; ' in pool and rut peel
    parches
Squandering ooze to squeezed ' dough, crust, dust;
    stanches, starches
Squadroned masks and manmarks ' treadmire toil there
Footfretted in it. Million-fuelèd, ' nature's bonfire
    burns on.
But quench her bonniest, dearest ' to her, her clearest-
    selvèd spark
Man, how fast his firedint, ' his mark on mind, is gone!
Both are in an unfathomable, all is in an enormous dark
Drowned. O pity and indig ' nation! Manshape, that
    shone

Sheer off, disseveral, a star, ' death blots black out; nor
    mark
                  Is any of him at all so stark
But vastness blurs and time ' beats level. Enough! the
    Resurrection,
A heart's-clarion! Away grief's gasping, ' joyless days,
    dejection.
                  Across my foundering deck shone
A beacon, an eternal beam. ' Flesh fade, and mortal
    trash
Fall to the residuary worm; ' world's wildfire, leave
    but ash:
                  In a flash, at a trumpet crash,
I am all at once what Christ is, ' since he was what
    I am, and
This Jack, joke, poor potsherd, ' patch, matchwood,
    immortal diamond,
                  Is immortal diamond.

in honour of

St Alphonsus Rodriguez

laybrother of the Society of Jesus

Honour is flashed off exploit, so we say;
And those strokes once that gashed flesh or galled shield
Should tongue that time now, trumpet now that field,
And, on the fighter, forge his glorious day.
On Christ they do and on the martyr may;
But be the war within, the brand we wield
Unseen, the heroic breast not outward-steeled,
Earth hears no hurtle then from fiercest fray.

Yet God (that hews mountain and continent,
Earth, all, out; who, with trickling increment,
Veins violets and tall trees makes more and more)
Could crowd career with conquest while there went
Those years and years by of world without event
That in Majorca Alfonso watched the door.

'Thou art indeed just, Lord'

Justus quidem tu es, Domine, si disputem tecum; verumtamen justa loquar ad te: Quare via impiorum prosperatur? &c.

Thou art indeed just, Lord, if I contend
With thee; but, sir, so what I plead is just.
Why do sinners' ways prosper? and why must
Disappointment all I endeavour end?

    Wert thou my enemy, O thou my friend,
How wouldst thou worse, I wonder, than thou dost
Defeat, thwart me? Oh, the sots and thralls of lust
Do in spare hours more thrive than I that spend,
Sir, life upon thy cause. See, banks and brakes
Now, leavèd how thick! lacèd they are again
With fretty chervil, look, and fresh wind shakes
Them; birds build – but not I build; no, but strain,
Time's eunuch, and not breed one work that wakes.
Mine, O thou lord of life, send my roots rain.

To R. B.

The fine delight that fathers thought; the strong
Spur, live and lancing like the blowpipe flame,
Breathes once and, quenchèd faster than it came,
Leaves yet the mind a mother of immortal song.
Nine months she then, nay years, nine years she long
Within her wears, bears, cares and combs the same:
The widow of an insight lost she lives, with aim
Now known and hand at work now never wrong.

    Sweet fire the sire of muse, my soul needs this;
I want the one rapture of an inspiration.
O then if in my lagging lines you miss
The roll, the rise, the carol, the creation,
My winter world, that scarcely breathes that bliss
Now, yields you, with some sighs, our explanation.

'Stars twiring brilliantly':
Extracts from Hopkins's Journals

May 3, 1866. Cold. Morning raw and wet, afternoon fine. Walked then with Addis, crossing Bablock Hythe, round by Skinner's Weir through many fields into the Witney Road. Sky sleepy blue without liquidity. Fr. Cumnor Hill saw St Philip's and the other spires through blue haze rising pale in a pink light. On further side of the Witney road hills, just fleeced with grain or other green growth, by their dips and waves foreshortened here and there and so differenced in brightness and opacity the green on them, with delicate effect. On left, brow of the near hill glistening with very bright newly turned sods and a scarf of vivid green slanting away beyond the skyline, agst. which the clouds shewed the slightest tinge of rose or purple. Copses in grey-red or grey-yellow – the tinges immediately forerunning the opening of full leaf. Meadows skirting Seven-bridge road voluptuous green. Some oaks are out in small leaf. Ashes not out, only tufted with their fringy blooms. Hedges springing richly. Elms in small leaf, with more or less opacity. White poplars most beautiful in small grey crisp spray-like leaf. Cowslips capriciously colouring meadows in creamy drifts. Bluebells, purple orchis. Over the green water of the river passing the slums of the town and under its bridges swallows shooting, blue and purple above and shewing their amber-tinged breasts reflected in the water, their flight unsteady with wagging wings and leaning first to one side then the other. Peewits flying. Towards sunset the sky partly swept, as often, with moist white cloud, tailing off across which are morsels of grey-black woolly clouds. Sun seemed to make a bright liquid hole in this, its texture had an upward northerly sweep or drift fr. the W. marked softly in grey. Dog violets. Eastward after sunset range of clouds rising in bulky heads moulded softly in tufts or bunches of snow – so it looks – and membered somewhat elaborately, rose-coloured. Notice often imperfect fairy rings. Apple and other fruit trees blossomed beautifully.

June 30. Thunderstorms all day, great claps and lightning running up and down. When it was bright betweentimes great towering clouds behind which the sun put out his shaded horns very clearly and a longish way. Level curds and whey sky after sunset. – Graceful growth of Etzkoltzias or however those unhappy flowers are spelt. Yews and evergreen trees now very thin and putting out their young pale shoots.

July 1. Sharp showers, bright between. Late in the afternoon, the light and shade being brilliant, snowy blocks of cloud were filing over the sky, and under the sun hanging above and along the earth-line were those multitudinous up-and-down crispy sparkling chains with pearly shadows up to the edges. At sunset, wh. was in a grey bank with moist gold dabs and racks, the whole round of skyline had level clouds naturally lead-colour but the upper parts ruddled, some more, some less, rosy. Spits or beams braided or built in with slanting pellet flakes made their way. Through such clouds anvil-shaped pink ones and up-blown fleece-of-wool flat-topped dangerous-looking pieces.

July 18. Bright. Sunset over oaks a dapple of rosy clouds blotted with purple, sky round confused pale green and blue with faint horned rays, crimson sparkles through the leaves below . . .

Aug. 30, 1867. Fair; in afternoon fine; the clouds had a good deal of crisping and mottling. – A round by Plumley. – Stands of ash in a copse: they consisted of two or three rods most gracefully leaved, for each wing or comb finally curled inwards, that is upwards. – Putting my hand up against the sky whilst we lay on the grass I saw more richness and beauty in the blue than I had known of before, not brilliance but glow and colour. It was not transparent and sapphire-like, but turquoise-like, swarming and blushing round the edge of the hand and in the pieces clipped in by the fingers, the flesh being sometimes sunlit, sometimes glassy with reflected light, sometimes lightly shadowed in that violet one makes with cobalt and Indian red.

July 3, 1868 . . . Started with Ed. Bond for Switzerland. We went by Dover and Ostende to Brussels . . .

July 9. Before sunrise looking out of window saw a noble scape of stars – the Plough all golden falling, Cassiopeïa on end with her bright quains pointing to the right, the graceful bends of Perseus underneath her, and some great star whether Capella or not I am not sure risen over the brow of the mountain. Sunrise we saw well: the north landscape was blighty but the south, the important one, with the Alps, clear; lower down all was mist and flue of white cloud, wh. grew thicker as the day went on and like a junket lay scattered on the lakes. The sun lit up the bright acres of the snows at first with pink but afterwards clear white: the snow of the Bernese Highland remained from its distance pinkish all day. – The mountain ranges, as any series or body of inanimate like things not often seen, have the air of persons and of interrupted activity; they are multitudinous too, and also they express a second level with an upper world or shires of snow. – In going down betw. Pilatus and a long streak of cloud the blue sky was greenish. Since I have found this colour is seen in looking fr. the snow to the sky but why I do not understand: can there possibly be a rose hue suppressed in the white (– *purpurea candidior nive*)?

July 11. Fine. We took a guide up the Wylerhorn but the top being clouded dismissed him and stayed up the mountain, lunching by a waterfall. Presently after long climbing – for there was a good chance of a clearance – we nearly reached the top, when a cloud coming on thick frightened me back: had we gone on we shd. have had the view, for it cleared quite. Still we saw the neighbouring mountains well. The snow is often cross-harrowed and lies too in the straightest paths as though artificial, wh. again comes fr. the planing. In the sheet it glistens yellow to the sun. How fond of and warped to the mountains it wd. be easy to become! For every cliff and limb and edge and jutty has its own nobility. – Two boys came down the mountain yodelling. – We saw the snow in the hollows for the first time. In one the surface was crisped across the direction of the cleft and the other way, that is across the broader crisping and down the stream, combed: the stream ran below and smoke came fr. the hollow: the edge of the snow hewn in curves as if by moulding planes. – Crowd of mountain flowers – gentians; gentianellas; blood-red lucerne; a deep blue glossy spiked flower like plantain, flowering gradually up the spike, so that at the top it looks like clover or honeysuckle; rich big harebells glistening black like the cases of our veins when dry and heated fr. without; and others. All the herbage enthronged with every fingered or fretted leaf. – Firs very tall, with the swell of the branching on the outer side of the slope so that the peaks seem to point inwards to the mountain peak, like the lines of the Parthenon, and the outline melodious and moving on many focuses. – I wore my pagharee and turned it with harebells below and gentians in two rows above like double pan-pipes. – In coming down we lost our way and each had a dangerous slide down the long wet grass of a steep slope.

Waterfalls not only skeined but silky too – one saw it fr. the inn across the meadows: at one quain of the rock the water glistened above and took shadow below, and the rock was reddened a little way each side with the wet, wh. sets off the silkiness . . .

July 19 [. . .] We saw Handeck waterfall. It is in fact the meeting of two waters, the right the Aar sallow and jade-coloured, the left a smaller stream of clear lilac foam. It is the greatest fall we have seen. The lower half is hidden in spray. I watched the great bushes of foam-water, the texture of branchings and water-spandrils which makes them up. At their outsides nearest the rock they gave off showers of drops strung together into little quills which sprang out in fans.

On crossing the Aar again there was as good a fall as some we have paid to see, all in jostling foam-bags.

Across the valley too we saw the fall of the Gelmer – like milk chasing round blocks of coal; or a girdle or long purse of white weighted with irregular black rubies, carelessly thrown aside and lying in jutty bends, with a black clasp of the same stone at the top – for those were the biggest blocks, squared, and built up, as it happened, in lessening stories, and the cascade enclosed them on the right and left hand with its foam; or once more like the skin of a white snake square-pied with black.

July 20. Fine.

Walked down to the Rhone glacier. It has three stages – first a smoothly-moulded bed in a pan or theatre of thorny peaks, swells of ice rising through the snow-sheet and the snow itself tossing and fretting into the sides of the rock walls in spray-like points: this is the first stage of the glaciers generally; it is like bright-plucked water swaying in a pail –; second, after a slope nearly covered with land-slips of moraine, was a ruck of horned waves steep and narrow in the gut: now in the upper Grindelwald glacier between the bed or highest stage was a descending limb which was like the rude and knotty bossings of a strombus shell –; third the foot, a broad limb opening out and reaching the plain, shaped like the fan-fin of a dolphin or a great bivalve shell turned on its face, the flutings in either case being suggested by the crevasses and the ribs by the risings between them, these being swerved and inscaped strictly to the motion of the mass. Or you may compare the three stages to the heel, instep, and ball or toes of a foot. – The second stage looked at from nearer appeared like a box of plaster of Paris or starch or tooth-powder a little moist, tilted up and then struck and jarred so that the powder broke and tumbled in shapes and rifts.

We went into the grotto and also the vault from which the Rhone flows. It looked like a blue tent and as you went further in changed to lilac. As you come out the daylight glazes the groins with gleaming rosecolour. The ice inside has a branchy wire texture. The man shewed us the odd way in which a little piece of ice will stick against the walls – as if drawn by a magnet.

Standing on the glacier saw the prismatic colours in the clouds, and worth saying what sort of clouds: it was fine shapeless skins of fretted make, full of eyebrows or like linings of curled leaves which one finds in shelved corners of a wood.

I had a trudge over the glacier and a tumble over the side moraine, which was one landslip of limestone. It was neighboured however by hot sweet smells and many flowers – small crimson pinks, the brown tulip-like flower we have seen so often, another which we first saw yesterday like Solomon's seal but rather coarser with a spike of greenish veiny-leaved blossom, etc.

July 24. Bright.
E. B. started in the night for the Cima di Jazzi; I stayed behind being ill.

At sunset great bulks of brassy cloud hanging round, which changed their colour to bright reds over the sundown and to fruittree-blossom colour opposite: later a honey-brown edged the Dent Blanche and Weisshorn ridge.

Note that a slender race of fine flue cloud inscaped in continuous eyebrow curves hitched on the Weisshorn peak as it passed: this shews the height of this kind of cloud, from its want of shadow etc. not otherwise discoverable.

July 25. But too bright.

Up at two to ascend the Breithorn. Stars twiring brilliantly. Taurus up, a pale light stressily edging the eastern skyline, and lighting mingled with the dawn. In the twilight we tumbled over the moraine and glacier until the sunrise brightly fleshed the snow of the Breithorn before us and then the colour changing through metallic shades of yellow recovered to white.

We were accompanied by a young Mr Pease of Darlington, his guide Gasser, and ours, Welchen.

From the summit the view on the Italian side was broken by endless ranges of part-vertical dancing cloud, the highest and furthest flaked or foiled like fungus and coloured pink. But, as the Interlaken Frenchman said, the mountain summits are not the places for mountain views, the things do not look high when you are as high as they are; besides Monte Rosa, the Lyskamm, etc. did not make themselves; shape as well as size went: then the cold feet, the spectacles, the talk, and the lunching came in. Even with one companion ecstasy is almost banished: you want to be alone and to feel that, and leisure – all pressure taken off.

March 12, 1870. A fine sunset: the higher sky dead clear blue bridged by a broad slant causeway rising from right to left of wisped or grass cloud, the wisps lying across; the sundown yellow, moist with light but ending at the top in a foam of delicate white pearling and spotted with big tufts of cloud in colour russet between brown and purple but edged with brassy light. But what I note it all for is this: before I had always taken the sunset and the sun as quite out of gauge with each other, as indeed physically they are, for the eye after looking at the sun is blunted to everything else and if you look at the rest of the sunset you must cover the sun, but today I inscaped them together and made the sun the true eye and ace of the whole, as it is. It was all active and tossing out light and started as strongly forward from the field as a long stone or a boss in the knop of the chalice-stem: it is indeed by stalling it so that it falls into scape with the sky.

The next morning a heavy fall of snow. It tufted and toed the firs and yews and went on to load them till they were taxed beyond their spring. The limes, elms, and Turkey-oaks it crisped beautifully as with young leaf. Looking at the elms from underneath you saw every wave in every twig (become by this the wire-like stem to a finger of snow) and to the hangers and flying sprays it restored, to the eye, the inscapes they had lost. They were beautifully brought out against the sky, which was on one side dead blue, on the other washed with gold.

Sept. 24. First saw the Northern Lights. My eye was caught by beams of light and dark very like the crown of horny rays the sun makes behind a cloud. At first I thought of silvery cloud until I saw that these were more luminous and did not dim the clearness of the stars in the Bear. They rose slightly radiating thrown out from the earthline. Then I saw soft pulses of light one after another rise and pass upwards arched in shape but waveringly and with the arch broken. They seemed to float, not following the warp of the sphere as falling stars look to do but free though concentrical with it. This busy working of nature wholly independent of the earth and seeming to go on in a strain of time not reckoned by our reckoning of days and years but simpler and as if correcting the preoccupation of the world by being preoccupied with and appealing to and dated to the day of judgement was like a new witness to God and filled me with delightful fear

April 22, 1871. But such a lovely damasking in the sky as today I never felt before. The blue was charged with simple instress, the higher, zenith sky earnest and frowning, lower more light and sweet. High up again, breathing through woolly coats of cloud or on the quains and branches of the flying pieces it was the true exchange of crimson, nearer the earth/ against the sun/ it was turquoise, and in the opposite south-western bay below the sun it was like clear oil but just as full of colour, shaken over with slanted flashing 'travellers', all in flight, stepping one behind the other, their edges tossed with bright ravelling, as if white napkins were thrown up in the sun but not quite at the same moment so that they were all in a scale down the air falling one after the other to the ground

May 9 . . . This day and May 11 the bluebells in the little wood between the College and the highroad and in one of the Hurst Green cloughs. In the little wood/ opposite the light/ they stood in blackish spreads or sheddings like the spots on a snake. The heads are then like thongs and solemn in grain and grape-colour. But in the clough/ through the light/ they came in falls of sky-colour washing the brows and slacks of the ground with vein-blue, thickening at the double, vertical themselves and the young grass and brake fern combed vertical, but the brake struck the upright of all this with light winged transomes. It was a lovely sight. – The bluebells in your hand baffle you with their inscape, made to every sense: if you draw your fingers through them they are lodged and struggle/ with a shock of wet heads; the long stalks rub and click and flatten to a fan on one another like your fingers themselves would when you passed the palms hard across one another, making a brittle rub and jostle like the noise of a hurdle strained by leaning against; then there is the faint honey smell and in the mouth the sweet gum when you bite them. But this is easy, it is the eye they baffle. They give one a fancy of pan-pipes and of some wind instrument with stops – a trombone perhaps. The over- hung necks – for growing they are little more than a staff with a simple crook but in water, where they stiffen, they take stronger turns, in the head like sheephooks or, when more waved throughout, like the waves riding through a whip that is being smacked – what with these overhung necks and what with the crisped ruffled bells dropping mostly on one side and the gloss these have at their foot-stalks they have an air of the knights at chess. Then the knot or 'knoop' of buds some shut, some just gaping, which makes the pencil of the whole spike, should be noticed: the inscape of the flower most finely carried out in the siding of the axes, each striking a greater and greater slant, is finished in these clustered buds, which for the most part are not straightened but rise to the end like a tongue and this and their tapering and a little flat-tening they have make them look like the heads of snakes.

Feb. 24, 1873. In the snow flat-topped hillocks and shoulders outlined with wavy edges, ridge below ridge, very like the grain of wood in line and in projection like relief maps. These the wind makes I think and of course drifts, which are in fact snow waves. The sharp nape of a drift is sometimes broken by slant flutes or channels. I think this must be when the wind after shaping the drift first has changed and cast waves in the body of the wave itself. All the world is full of inscape and chance left free to act falls into an order as well as purpose: looking out of my window I caught it in the random clods and broken heaps of snow made by the cast of a broom. The same of the path trenched by footsteps in ankledeep snow across the fields leading to Hodder wood through which we went to see the river. The sun was bright, the broken brambles and all boughs and banks limed and cloyed with white, the brook down the clough pulling its way by drops and by bubbles in turn under a shell of ice

In March there was much snow

April 8. The ashtree growing in the corner of the garden was felled. It was lopped first: I heard the sound and looking out and seeing it maimed there came at that moment a great pang and I wished to die and not to see the inscapes of the world destroyed any more